One SMILE, One ARM

Many smiles to you!
Becky ☺

One SMILE, One ARM

Life Experiences with One Arm

BECKY ALEXANDER

WESTBOW
PRESS
A DIVISION OF THOMAS NELSON

WestBow Press books may be ordered through booksellers or by contacting:

WestBow Press
A Division of Thomas Nelson
1663 Liberty Drive
Bloomington, IN 47403
www.westbowpress.com
1-(866) 928-1240

ISBN: 978-1-4497-9605-1 (sc)
ISBN: 978-1-4497-9606-8 (hc)
ISBN: 978-1-4497-9604-4 (e)
Library of Congress Control Number: 2013909252

Printed in the United States of America.

WestBow Press rev. date: 05/31/2013

I dedicate this book to my parents,
Mark and Truby Selby,
who taught a little handicapped girl that
she was not handicapped at all.

CONTENTS

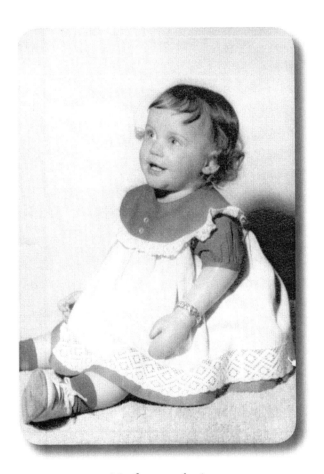

My first prosthesis

JFK

MY LEFT SIDE was messed up at birth. My leg turned inward, and I had no elbow, forearm, or hand. The doctor put a cast on my leg that led to my hip, which I wore for the first three months of my life. I learned to roll over by tossing the cast across my other leg, which would then flip me over. Thankfully, the casting procedure worked; my leg straightened out, and I had no further problems with it.

Mom quickly began the pursuit of a prosthetic arm for me. She learned that a prescription was required to start the process. When she asked the pediatrician for one, his response caught her off guard.

"No," he stated. "You need to let Becky get old enough to decide for herself if she wants a prosthesis."

Mom didn't agree. She felt that my getting a prosthesis as an infant would make it easier for me to get used to it and would help me as I developed life skills. She went to another doctor who surprisingly told her the same thing. So she went to a third doctor and a fourth doctor. Neither of them would grant her a prescription. It was obvious that the popular opinion in the medical field discouraged infant prostheses. Mom was frustrated but not willing to give up. She sat down at the kitchen table and wrote a letter to the president of the United States of America!

The year was 1961. John F. Kennedy was in office. Lucky for me, President Kennedy was involved in helping crippled children across the country. He responded to Mom's letter almost immediately. Now I'm sure the president didn't type the letter himself, but it came from his administration. They connected Mom with the Crippled Children's Foundation, who ultimately got her the prescription she needed. On February 5, 1962 (my first birthday), I had an appointment at a prosthetics facility in Grand Rapids, Michigan. One month later, I was wearing my first prosthetic arm.

Today, specialists in the field of pediatric prosthetics recommend that children be fitted for prostheses as early as six months old. I'm glad Mom knew what was best for me even though it differed from the thinking of the medical community. My prosthesis has allowed me to live a normal, high-functioning life with few limitations. And it's all thanks to Mom and JFK!

"Be strong and do not give up, for
your work will be rewarded"
(2 Chronicles 15:7 NIV).

SOCIAL SECURITY ADMINISTRATION
433 West Van Buren Street - Room 712   June 16, 1961

Mrs. Mark Selby
R. R. 1
West Middletown, Ohio

Dear Mrs. Selby:

Your letter addressed to President John F. Kennedy has been referred to me for reply. I was sorry to hear about Rebecca but also very pleased about your interest in having her fitted with an artificial arm. We do find that the sooner a child like this is fitted the easier it is for her to use it. I am sending you our Children's Bureau pamphlet "The Child with a Missing Arm or Leg" and another pamphlet prepared by the Michigan Area Amputee Center which I hope will be helpful to you.

Under the provisions of the Social Security Act, Federal grant-in-aids are made available to the States for the care of children with certain handicapping conditions whose parents are unable to pay for the full cost of care. Usually children such as Rebecca are covered under these programs. In Ohio the State agency receiving these funds is Services for Crippled Children, State Department of Public Welfare, Columbus, Ohio, and Miss Mildred Smith is the Administrator. I would suggest that you get in touch with Miss Smith about your daughter and I am sure that she or a member of her staff could be helpful to you. I am taking the privilege of sending a copy of your letter to Miss Smith and to Mrs. Ruth Winters, Social Work Consultant.

I hope that this letter will be helpful to you.

Sincerely yours,

John M. Saunders

John M. Saunders, M.D.
Acting Regional Medical Director
Children's Bureau

Enclosures (2)

4

NEW WATCH

ONE OF THE biggest events in my life happened in second grade. I got my first prosthetic hand! Up until then, I had always worn a hook. I was so proud of my new hand. It looked extremely real. I couldn't wait to wear it to school. My papaw, Otto, even bought me a brand new watch to wear on my arm.

Monday finally came. You know those days when you can't quit smiling? It was one of those days. The kids on the bus were fascinated with my new hand. They asked me questions about it all the way to school. I bounced off the bus and headed to my class. The kids in my class were excited too. They wanted to touch my new hand and see me operate it. When the bell rang, we all took our seats. My teacher Mrs. Rickey[1] walked over

---

1   Mrs. Rickey's name was changed to protect the guilty and the dead.

to my desk. I was beaming. I expected her to compliment my new hand and ask me about it. Instead, she coldly said, "You're wearing that watch on the wrong hand. You're supposed to wear a watch on the right hand." Then she walked away.

I was confused. *I didn't know there is a rule about which hand you're supposed to wear a watch on,* I thought. *And she didn't say a word about my new hand. Maybe she didn't notice it.*

When I got home from school, I told my mom what Mrs. Rickey said. Mom seemed instantly mad and assured me that I could wear a watch on whichever hand I'd like.

Looking back on that day, I'm amazed. Aren't teachers called to encourage, build up, and inspire students? What was Mrs. Rickey doing? Was she trying to kill my joy? Why would she do that to a kid? It's a good thing for Mrs. Rickey that she made the comment to seven-year-old Becky and not to fifty-two-year-old Becky, for fifty-two-year-old Becky would give her a few pointers on how to treat children. Mrs. Rickey would probably start wearing her watch on her left hand.

"Better to wear a millstone necklace and take
a swim in the deep blue sea than give even one
of these dear little ones a hard time!"
(Luke 17:2 MSG).

Seven-year-old Becky

GIRL FIGHT

THE CLOSEST I ever came to getting in a fight was with a girl named Vickie Carmichael. She wasn't much bigger than I was, but she was tough. Everybody feared her in fifth-grade gym class when we played dodgeball. And she had her eye on me. I'm not sure why. Maybe my prosthetic left arm made me a target. Kids like to pick on kids who are different in some way—kids without stylish clothes, kids who are overweight, kids with disabilities, new kids.

It always happened after school on the way to the bus. I dreaded the walk along the long line of yellow school buses because there was no hiding from Vickie. She spotted me every day. I froze in my tracks when I saw her and braced for the pain. She made a fist, pulled it back behind her head, and full-force punched me in my upper right arm. I didn't cry. I simply took it and then got on the bus. I never told anybody. I just lived in fear of Vickie Carmichael.

For months, I contemplated my lot in life, a victim of Vickie Carmichael. I knew something had to change. I decided I had to fight back, so I devised a plan. I wasn't convinced it would work, but I was determined to try it. Then one day, I put my plan into action.

Vickie approached me as usual. My heart pounded. I had to act before she did. I took a deep breath and gathered my courage. Then I drew back my purse and hit Vickie Carmichael with it as hard as I could. I spun around and ran for my life toward the bus. I fully expected to die that day. But surprisingly, Vickie didn't chase me. In fact, she never hit me again.

Courage isn't the absence of fear. It's facing the enemy in spite of our fear. I realized that day that I could be courageous. I've had to be courageous many times in the years since. So if you ever find yourself facing an enemy and needing courage, call me. I'll come over with my purse.

"Be strong and courageous. Do not be afraid;
do not be discouraged, for the Lord your God
will be with you wherever you go"
(Joshua 1:9 NIV).

Skating Rink

I started to roller skate with my family when I was in elementary school. Dad and Mom were great skaters. I remember watching them do the Boogie Bounce to the live organ music. Dad often showed off, spinning and doing fancy footwork. I became a pretty good skater myself by fifth grade. I even owned my own white skates with purple pom-poms.

One evening, I was dancing around the skating rink to "Knock Three Times" when this older kid came whizzing past me. His skate accidentally clipped my skate and I lost my balance. I took a hard tumble and landed on my right wrist. A floor guard named Bob[2] reached me within seconds.

---

2   I found out years later that Floor Guard Bob was Bob Alexander—my future father-in-law. Ain't life funny?

"We need to get you off the floor before someone runs into you," he said.

I nodded through my tears. He scooped me up in his arms and glided me off the floor.

By the next morning, my wrist was badly swollen. Mom announced, "No school for you today. We're going to get that wrist X-rayed. It could be broken."

Broken? A broken bone sounded really scary. "If it's broken, what will happen?" I asked.

"The doctor will probably put a cast on your arm," Mom explained.

A cast that all my friends could sign? *That* made me smile. Mom helped me dress, and we headed to the emergency room.

Luckily, the ER wasn't too busy. An attendant promptly escorted us to one of the curtained sections of the exam room. I climbed up on the bed while a nurse asked Mom about the injury. She made some notes inside a metal chart, slammed it shut, and said as she slipped out the curtain, "The doctor will be in to see you in a few minutes."

We waited and waited and waited. Mom told me you always have to wait a long time in an emergency room. Finally, the curtain jerked open and a doctor entered. He gently examined my wrist, and I winced when he turned it right or left. By the look on his face, I suspected that I might get a cast.

"Let's take you to X-ray and see what's going on with this wrist," he stated. Then he quickly walked out, jerking the curtain shut behind him.

Well, the X-ray confirmed it—my wrist was broken. The doctor put on a cast from my knuckles to my elbow! It was kind of fun at first—showing up at school wearing a cast, letting everybody sign it with a black marker, and kids offering to carry my lunch tray and books. But it didn't take long for the fun to wear off. With one prosthetic arm and the other in a cast, even the simplest tasks were a challenge. My teachers had to give me tests orally because I couldn't write. Mom had to wash my hair and assist me with baths. And the worst part of all was that I couldn't go to the skating rink for five weeks!

---⊗⊗⊗---

"Have mercy on me, Lord, for I am faint; heal
me, Lord, for my bones are in agony"
(Psalm 6:2 NIV).

---⊗⊗⊗---

THE OGRE

IKE MOST OF you, on the day I turned sixteen I was at the license exam station taking my driving test. I was quite nervous because I had heard all the stories about the ogre who administered the test in Butler County. But he wasn't so bad and I passed with no problems.

A woman at the desk snapped my picture before giving me a chance to arrange my hair or smile. She printed my temporary license and handed it to me. I was a licensed driver! I walked away slowly reading every word:

» REBECCA GAIL SELBY

» 7463 GERMANTOWN RD

» MIDDLETOWN, OH 45042

» SEX F

- » HT 4-11
- » WT 95
- » EYES BLU
- » HAIR BRO
- » RESTRICTIONS PA

I stopped. Restrictions? No way! I turned around and marched back to the woman at the desk.

"What do the P and A after the word *Restrictions* mean?" I questioned.

She explained, "Because of your arm, the examiner feels it would be best if you only drive a vehicle with power steering or a spinner knob. That's what the P indicates. The A means automatic shift. He thinks you need that too."

I wasn't happy. I could accept the P. Steering into tight spots without power steering was difficult with one arm. But the A—that one was not acceptable. My dad's jeep was a stick shift, and I knew I could drive it. My friend Donna had a stick shift and I drove it too. No, this restriction was going to cramp me. My eyes searched the office for the ogre. There he was. I approached him and ever so sweetly but boldly asked, "If I can pass the driving test in a stick shift, will you remove this A from my license?"

He looked surprised. He thought for a moment and then replied, "Yes, young lady, I'm willing to consider that."

I left the exam station and headed to Donna's house to borrow her red Toyota. After a few practice runs around the block, I returned to the station to retake the test. The ogre almost smiled when he saw me coming. "That was fast!" he exclaimed. "Let's see what you can do."

I passed. The examiner removed the A. I decided he wasn't such an ogre after all.

Everyone deals with restrictions in life. Some restrictions are Ps—justified and necessary for our own good or the good of others. Other restrictions are As—unjustified and imposed upon us by ogres. Here's my advice: graciously and respectfully accept the Ps, but fight with all you have to remove the As.

"Christ has set us free to live a free life. So take your stand!
Never again let anyone put a harness of slavery on you"
(Galatians 5:1 MSG).

Bionic Woman

(To set the scene, it was 1977. Two of the most popular shows on TV were *The Six Million Dollar Man* and *The Bionic Woman*.)

A MONG MY MANY adventures in life was a run as a singer in a country band. We called ourselves The Country Breeze. We were quite famous in our small Ohio town. On weekdays, we dissected frogs in biology class, participated in extracurricular activities, hung out with friends, and ate lots of foot long chili dogs at the root beer stand. But on weekends, we hit the stage.

We were pretty good for high school kids. My sister Cindy played guitar and sang lead. Because she couldn't harmonize, I always sang the harmonies. Our voices sounded almost the same so they blended well. Mike Barker played bass and his brother Mark Barker played banjo. Mark could make a banjo dance on "Cripple Creek," "Dueling Banjos," and "Rocky Top." Jeff Baker was our drummer, and my dad was our sound guy.

One weekend we were playing at the Honey Festival in Lebanon, Ohio. We had just kicked off "Rocky Mountain High" when a little girl in the audience yelled, "What's wrong with your arm?" I ignored her and kept singing. A few minutes passed and she yelled again, "What's wrong with your arm?"

I thought, *Where are her parents? Why are they letting her do that?* At sixteen, I was highly embarrassed. When the song ended, I motioned for the girl to come to the edge of the stage. I patiently explained to her that I was born with one arm and that I was wearing a prosthetic arm to help me do things. She seemed satisfied. She walked back into the crowd, and we kicked off our next song.

Two minutes later, I heard very loudly, "What's wrong with your arm?" As I continued to sing, I watched my boyfriend, Tim (now my husband), weave his way through the crowd to the little girl. He bent down and said something in her ear. She slowly looked up at him, and then she slowly looked toward the stage at me. She never said another word.

The Country Breeze performed a few more songs before taking a honey ice cream break. When Tim walked over to join me, I exclaimed, "Thanks for making that little girl shut up! What did you tell her?"

He smiled and answered, "I told her you are the Bionic Woman and I am the Six Million Dollar Man and she better be quiet."

---❀❀❀---

"Love always protects"
(1 Corinthians 13:7 NIV).

---❀❀❀---

The Country Breeze
Left to right: Mark, Cindy, Jeff, Becky, Mike

CUSTARD-FILLED DOUGHNUTS

M Y FIRST JOB was at a bakery in the Towne Mall. It was a small place with one set of lit glass display cases. Shoppers stared at the custard-filled doughnuts, coconut macaroons, and apple fritters as they passed by. I was especially drawn to the custard-filled doughnuts.

I was a high school junior and worked the after-school shift. Friends waved or stopped to talk for a minute or two on their way to other stores. I greeted customers with a smile, filled their orders, kept the cases fully stocked, and packed the goodies away at closing.

Soon I noticed that the longer a person worked at the bakery the more responsibilities he or she was awarded. I watched as other teens baked the coconut macaroons, glazed the apple fritters, and filled the doughnuts with custard. I looked forward to the day when I would get to move up the corporate ladder.

As the weeks passed, I observed a coworker with less seniority than me getting to fill the doughnuts with custard. I kept smiling, greeting customers, and restocking the glass cases, but the manager never asked me to fill the doughnuts with custard. One night at closing, I casually said to my coworker, "I wonder when I'll get to fill the doughnuts with custard?"

Freeze time. I was seventeen. I had the highest GPA in the class of '79 at Madison High School. I could wiggle with the best of them on the drill team in the Mohawk marching band. I was emerging as a leader as president of the junior class. I was singing at weekend gigs with The Country Breeze Band. I was riding my Honda 90, waterskiing, and dating. I had no limitations, and the world was before me.

Unfreeze time. My coworker replied, "The owner says you can't fill the doughnuts with custard because you only have one arm."

I looked at her blankly and blurted, "What?"

Confused, I replayed the words in my head. I couldn't process them.

I struggled, "What does my arm have to do with custard-filled doughnuts?" I simply could not make the connection.

In that one unexpected moment, I was introduced to the rest of my life.

———∞∞∞———

"We are hard pressed on every side, but not crushed;
perplexed, but not in despair; persecuted, but not
abandoned; struck down, but not destroyed"
(2 Corinthians 4:8–9 NIV).

———∞∞∞———

FRIDAY NIGHT LIGHTS

I WAS AT EVERY high school football game for four years, but I don't think I ever watched one. Football games weren't about football. They were about putting on those shiny Sheer Energy pantyhose, white boots with red pom-poms, a red and white uniform with a short skirt, and red tights underneath. They were about dancing crazy on the sidelines while the band played. They were about shivering under blankets on cold Ohio nights and drinking hot chocolate from the concession stand. They were about walking around with boyfriends during third quarter. And they were definitely about the halftime show.

As a member of the drill team in the Mohawk marching band, I took the field each Friday night alongside my fifteen comrades. We performed to songs like "S-A-T-U-R-D-A-Y Night," "The Rockford Files," and "Do the Hustle." Usually, we used shakers for our routines. That worked great for me, because I could hold a shaker in my prosthetic left hand and no one knew the difference. I'd practice while watching my reflection in the porch windows of my house to make sure the movements with my left arm looked the same as the movements with my right arm. All was well until *the red and white gloves.*

Beth, our captain, announced that we would be wearing some really cool gloves for our next routine. She pulled a pair out of her purse and put them on to show us. They were white on the back and red on the palm.

"At various points in the routine we will flash all white," Beth explained. "At other points we will flash all red."

When Beth demonstrated, my heart sank. I knew I couldn't do that. My prosthetic hand would only open and close; it wouldn't rotate at the wrist and the fingers wouldn't straighten out.

I discussed the situation with Dad at supper. "I've never had to sit out of a game before, but I'm going to have to this time," I told him.

He scrunched his forehead and said, "Don't give up just yet. Let me think about it."

Dad went to work that night at Armco Steel. He shared my dilemma with his fellow machinists. They spent their break time brainstorming possible solutions. As they talked about the need for wrist rotation, a man named Gene Brown speculated, "What about an ice cream scooper? You know, the kind that you push the lever and the piece slides across the inside of the scoop. I wonder if we could use that rotating mechanism somehow."

Dad and the other guys became quiet and considered how

that might work. "You could be on to something there, Gene," Dad replied.

"I've got one at home," Gene added. "I'll bring it tomorrow."

And that's how it happened.

Dad and his friends connected the rotating mechanism from the ice cream scooper to my prosthetic wrist and cabling. Then they fashioned straight "fingers" from strips of metal, padded around them, and pulled my red and white glove over them. It looked like a hand. The movements that previously opened and closed my hand amazingly rotated it from red to white!

I don't remember if the Madison Mohawks won the football game that Friday night. I can't name the quarterback or the most valuable player. But of one thing I am very sure—my dad was the star of the game.

―――ᴏᴇᴇᴏ―――

"As a father has compassion on his children, so the Lord has compassion on those who fear him" (Psalm 103:13 NIV).

―――ᴏᴇᴇᴏ―――

CRUSHED

I RECEIVE MANY COMMENTS about my prosthetic left arm. Some are kind, encouraging, inspiring. Some are borderline, awkward, puzzling. Some are irritating, mouth dropping, even abusive—like the comment from a stranger in Target who crushed my teenage heart.

I had just finished my four-hour shift in the shoe department. I was feeling good. It was payday *and* I had a date in a few hours. I decided to try on the pair of purple heels I had been eyeing all morning. They would perfectly match my new purple skirt. I slipped on the right shoe and admired it in the floor mirror. As I bent down to put on the left shoe, an older woman suddenly appeared next to me. I glanced up at her and she began to speak.

"What happened to your arm?" she asked bluntly.

I smiled and answered, "I was born with one arm."

The woman didn't smile back. She just stared at my arm as I straightened up. When she finally spoke again, she said bitterly, "Well, someone in your family must have done something really bad for you to have been born with an arm like that." Then she turned quickly and strutted out of the shoe department.

I stood motionless in the purple heels watching her walk away. My arm a punishment? That idea had never entered my mind. My parents had always told me I was special, that God had made me the way I am for a reason. I had never questioned it. How could that woman say such a horrible thing?

A few weeks later, I was reading my Bible and stumbled upon the most amazing story. I couldn't believe what I was reading. It was as if Jesus was speaking directly to my crushed heart. Here's what it said:

As Jesus went along, he saw a man blind from birth. His disciples asked him, "Rabbi, who sinned, this man, or his parents, that he was born blind?"

"Neither this man nor his parents sinned," said Jesus, "but this happened so that the work of God might be displayed in his life" (John 9:1–3 NIV).

Wow. Jesus set the record straight for me. I defiantly tossed that woman's poisoned words out of my mind and never allowed them to hurt me again.

―――∞∞∞――

"Words kill, words give life; they're either
poison or fruit—you choose"
(Proverbs 18:21 MSG).

―――∞∞∞――

PRISSY GIRLS

I WAS IN A pageant—once. I'm not sure why I entered. Maybe because it was something I hadn't tried before, and I like to try most everything once. I was a contestant in the Junior Miss Pageant of Butler County, Ohio, in December of 1978.

Oh, my gosh. I hated it. I had never seen so many prissy girls in all my life. I don't like prissy girls.

Fitness was a scoring category. We were judged on physical stamina, agility, and flexibility. They made us dance to *The Nutcracker*. I could dance just fine, just not a prissy dance, which was what they wanted us to do.

Self-expression was another scoring category. We were judged on poise, demeanor, and carriage. In other words, how prissy we were. We had to wear a long, white, sleeveless dress while parading across the stage in front of the judges. I don't do sleeveless. Sleeveless shows too many cables, bolts, and straps on my prosthetic left arm. My mom and I contacted the pageant organizers and asked if I could possibly wear a dress with three-quarter length sleeves. They were understanding and allowed me the option. The prissy girls were not happy. They said it wasn't fair and that it made me stand out from the other girls to the judges. I really don't like prissy girls.

The remaining three categories were less painful. I topped the Scholastics category with a 4.0 GPA. For the Talent category, I sang a Donna Fargo song called "United States of America." The judges seemed to enjoy the only non-prissy performance in the pageant. And I held my own in the private Interview category.

I didn't place in the pageant. I'm sure my joy of participating and my wonderful attitude toward the event shined like the Christmas tree on the stage. However, I learned a few things from the experience. First, never enter another pageant. Second, never shake your hips really big when you walk—it looks stupid. Third, when you have a daughter of your own, never let her grow up to be a prissy girl.

"The Lord does not look at the things man
looks at. Man looks at the outward appearance,
but the Lord looks at the heart"
(1 Samuel 16:7 NIV).

iPod Arm

THE UTAH MYOELECTRIC Arm became available in 1981 and shortly thereafter, I got one. It cost twenty-seven thousand dollars! Thankfully, my insurance covered most of it. The arm had an electric elbow and an electric hand, both powered by rechargeable battery packs. It was like *Back to the Future*.

My existing upper arm slid into a socket held on by suction. Within the socket were electrodes strategically placed to pick up signals from muscle contractions. When I flexed my front muscle, the elbow raised the forearm. When I flexed my back muscle, the elbow lowered the forearm. When I flexed the front and back muscles simultaneously, the elbow locked in its present position. (Confused yet? Hang on. There's more.) Once the elbow locked, I flexed the front muscle to open the hand and the back muscle to close the hand. It took serious concentration and lots of practice. (I challenge you to try it.

See if you can flex your front and back upper arm muscles separately.)

Because the arm was in the early stages of development, it had some issues. It was extremely heavy, the electric motors were loud, the battery packs ran down quickly, and the elbow and hand movements were slow. Also, I didn't always have full control of the movements. Let me try to explain. When a person bends over to pick something up, she doesn't let her arms fall freely forward, she holds them back using her upper arm muscles. Since my upper arm muscles connected to electrodes, my hand would start opening and closing. On another occasion, my hand began operating when I walked under some power lines. That lack of control was the biggest issue for me. After many months of effort, I chose to go back to a cable-operated arm.

Huge advancements have been made in the thirty years following my myoelectric arm. There is now a Utah Arm 2 and a Utah Arm 3 (U2 and U3 for short). Elbows and hands operate via tiny microcomputers. Electric wrists rotate 360 degrees. You can even get an arm that has a built-in iPod shuffle with stereo speakers! I really need one of those. I wonder if my insurance company would go for it.

"With your well-muscled arm and your grip
of steel—nobody trifles with you!"
(Psalm 89:13 MSG).

DUMBEST QUESTION

I HAVE BEEN ASKED a million questions in my lifetime. The most frequent one is, "What's wrong with your arm?" When I'm in my usual good mood, I smile and say, "I was born with one arm." When I'm in a particularly ornery mood, I have to restrain myself from responding, "What's wrong with your nose?" I've never done that, but I chuckle thinking about it. Please understand. I don't mind inquiries from family and friends. And I don't mind inquiries from kids—after all, I was a kids' pastor for twenty years. However, when a total stranger walks up to me in Walmart and asks me a very personal question, I have to admit, it agitates me a bit.

Then there's the "How do you _____?" question. Just fill in the blank with anything you'd like, I'm sure I've heard it.

On one occasion, I was at an airport with my daughter,

Cassie, who was five at the time. A little boy about the same age struck up a conversation with us. It went something like this: "How do you drive? How do you cook? How do you take a shower? How do you tie your shoes? How do you swim? How do you carry stuff?" It was like talking to Dennis the Menace. He hardly took a breath between segments of the interrogation. With each additional question, Cassie grew noticeably more aggravated. Finally, after the sixth question, she grabbed my right elbow and pulled my real hand out of my pocket. She shoved my hand about four inches from the boy's face and gave him the "duh" look.

But of all the questions I've ever been asked, this one is ultimately and eternally the dumbest, "Are you left-handed or right-handed?"

When someone asks that, all I can do is stare at him or her for a few seconds, my head cocked to one side, and my mouth slightly open. I mean, if I *were* left-handed, how would I know? I work hard to get out the words "right-handed" without making a funny face. I just flat gave up when one woman replied, "Well, it's a good thing!"

No matter how many times I am presented with the dumbest question (and you'd be surprised at the number), it always catches me off guard. So I decided to come up with a creative, predetermined answer. I discussed it with my brother-in-law Phillip, and he thought of the perfect retort. To the next person who asks, "Are you left-handed or right-handed?" I am going to respond, "I'm ambidextrous!"

"Do not let your left hand know what
your right hand is doing"
(Matthew 6:3 NIV).

FIRE AT SEA

TRAVEL IS ONE of life's great adventures. I've experienced a 675-mile yard sale, slept in a top of a castle in Germany, ridden a prop plane through a tornado in North Dakota, and accidentally took my family to a topless beach in Mexico. I stood on a mountain in Vermont that inspired *The Sound of Music*, and stayed in a creepy, abandoned hospital overlooking the Hollywood sign in California.

When travel involves flying, the adventure escalates. My prosthetic left arm sets off all kinds of alarms going through security checkpoints. I am scanned by a hand-held metal detector and patted down just like on *Law and Order*. Since 9/11, I am even swabbed for explosives. Officers wipe down the shoulder and hand of my prosthetic arm, and then test the swab using an explosive trace detection machine.

I must say my greatest travel adventure was a fire at sea. My family of four was in a small cabin on the Carnival cruise ship *Fantasy*. I was in the shower while the kids were getting dressed for dinner. My husband, Tim, needed to iron his shirt, so he unplugged the TV from the 220-volt outlet and plugged in the 110-volt iron. A few seconds later, he tapped on the bathroom door and said, "Beck, I think we've got a problem." I stuck my head out the door into a smoke-filled room.

"Get the kids out!" I screamed.

I grabbed the only piece of clothing in sight, a jacket, and pulled it on as I ran into the hall calling for the cabin steward. He appeared immediately. He took one look at the smoke rolling out of our cabin and raced for help. Within seconds, white uniforms were everywhere; they were running up and down the hall and in and out of our cabin. The four of us stood in shock watching from the hallway. Then suddenly I gasped—I was naked except for a very short jacket! I backed against the wall and stood statue-still for the next hour.

The crew eventually resolved the problem, and we returned to our cabin. The fire didn't kill my husband, but I wanted to.

June is my next travel adventure. Tim and I are going on a Hawaii cruise to Honolulu, Maui, Hilo, Kona, and Kauai on the ship *Pride of America*. You had better believe that I've already checked—the outlets are 110.

———∞———

"I came that they may have and enjoy life, and have
it in abundance (to the full, till it overflows)"
(John 10:10 AMP).

———∞———

1999

CAPITOL HILL

M Y COUSIN SERVES Alabama's Fourth Congressional District in the United States House of Representatives. In January of 2001, Robert Aderholt was being sworn into his third term of office. My mom, Truby, my daughter, Cassie, many cousins, and I flew to Washington, DC to celebrate with him at his office in Longworth House on Capitol Hill.

Robert gave us a behind-the-scenes tour of the United States Capitol. What an amazing place! The circular rotunda is where eleven presidents have lain in state, including Abraham Lincoln, John F. Kennedy, and Ronald Reagan. We climbed the 365-step staircase from the crypt under the rotunda to the top of the dome above the rotunda. Did you know there is a walkway on the *outside* around the top of the dome? I was too afraid to do anything but peek out the door.

The North Wing of the Capitol is home to the Senate

chamber. Though we were not allowed to touch anything, we were able to walk onto the Senate floor. The South Wing is the House of Representatives chamber. Our family had one seat in the gallery, which overlooked the House floor. We each were able to observe for fifteen minutes. During my fifteen minutes, the Speaker of the House, Dennis Hastert, was presented!

We traveled between the capitol buildings through underground tunnels on electric subway cars. At every stop on our tour, we went through a security checkpoint. And at every security checkpoint, the metal in my prosthetic elbow, wrist, and hand set off the alarms. The tour would stop while everyone waited for me to be scanned by a hand-held metal detector and patted down. Once was fine. Twice was okay. The third time I was embarrassed. The fourth time I felt humiliated. Then Robert walked over to me, put his arm around my shoulders, looked at the security guard, and said, "She's with me." From that point on, he and I walked through each checkpoint together.

There is a quote by Daniel Webster etched in marble on the wall of the House of Representatives. It reads, "Let us develop the resources of our land, call forth its powers, build up its institutions, promote all its great interests, and see whether we also, in our day and generation, may not perform something worthy to be remembered."

In my book of life, Robert has done that.

"Clothe yourselves with compassion, kindness, humility, gentleness, and patience" (Colossians 3:12 NIV).

GREEN FINGERNAILS

GREEN. I LIKE green. Especially lime green. Actually, I enjoy all lively colors as is obvious with a glance in my clothes closet. (Today, I'm wearing a daffodil-yellow fleece jacket.) A peek at my shoe collection further confirms it: turquoise moccasins, graffiti Converses, khaki hiking boots with purple and pink accents, tie-dye Reeboks, and pink boots. But it's not only my clothes and shoes. I drive an electric blue car. My bedroom is pink and orange. My office is orange and lime green. And I have a hot-pink stripe in my hair. As I said, I really like bright colors.

So when my daughter, Cassie, twelve at the time, asked me to paint my fingernails lime green like hers for St. Patrick's Day, I was all for it. My prosthetic left hand was a conglomeration of mechanical parts covered by a realistic-looking glove made of silicone. I didn't know if polish would adhere to the rubbery surface. I tediously painted each nail and it stuck! Then I held the handle of the polish brush in my mouth and painted the nails on my right hand. (Try it. I dare you!) Both hands turned out beautifully.

Cassie and I celebrated St. Patrick's Day by sporting our pretty lime green fingernails. She got lots of attention at West Morgan Middle School, and I received several raised eyebrows on my job at First Baptist Church. I loved it. The fun and the polish lasted a few days and then the polish began to chip off. I located the polish remover, dabbed some on a square of cotton, and swiped the nails on my prosthetic hand. Almost immediately, I knew something wasn't right. The green polish was coming off, but the green color wasn't. I gasped as I realized the polish had stained my silicone glove. My fingernails were permanently an ugly shade of yellow-green! I felt sick deep down in my stomach. Gloves cost four hundred dollars, and I had just ruined mine with lime green fingernail polish.

"There before me was a throne in heaven with someone sitting on it. And the one who sat there had the appearance of jasper and carnelian. A rainbow, resembling an emerald, encircled the throne" (Revelation 4:2–3 NIV).

THE BIRDCAGE

CHILDREN'S MINISTRY CHANGED a ton during the twenty years I worked in it. What started as flannel boards with little flannel people became stage, lights, and technology. The methods changed, but the message didn't.

Somewhere between flannel boards and technology, children's sermons were the thing. All the kids would come to the front of the church auditorium during the adult service, and I'd present a creative, five-minute object lesson. It was during one of these children's sermons that this event occurred.

The lesson was a tough one—death. I was on my knees so that I'd be on the same level as the kids. I was wearing my yellow ruffled skirt. I had lots of stuff—a huge birdcage, my pink Bible, and a bright yellow bucket full of candy bars to give to the kids as they returned to their seats.

"Imagine that you are a little yellow bird," I began, holding

63 §

the birdcage. "This big gold cage is your home. You have everything you need in this cage. You have a food dish, a mirror, and a swing. Then one day a little girl carries your cage into a rainforest. Splashes of sunlight, tall green trees, sweet-smelling flowers, and sparkling waterfalls surround your cage. And flying everywhere are thousands of birds." I paused and then asked slowly, "Can you imagine wanting to stay in this cage? It is comfortable. It is familiar. But it can't compare to the magnificent rainforest."

I explained that life here on earth is very similar. We have everything we need. It is comfortable and familiar. But it can't compare to what heaven is like. I concluded with a Bible verse, handed out the candy, and dismissed the kids to their seats.

At that moment, something snapped. At first, I wasn't sure what it was. Then I realized it was the elastic in the waist of my skirt. "Okay," my mind calculated. "How am I going to get up off my knees, hold my skirt, which is already slipping down my hips, carry the birdcage, my Bible, and the bucket, make it to the front row to sit down, and do it all with one hand?"

Six hundred people and a TV camera awaited my answer.

With all eyes on me, I pressed my prosthetic elbow hard against my hip to keep my skirt from slipping any lower. I positioned the birdcage on the stage for decoration. I grabbed my Bible and the bucket with my real hand, stood up, and made a mad dash for the front row. I made it.

"No eye has seen, no ear has heard, no mind has conceived
what God has prepared for those who love him"
(1 Corinthians 2:9 NIV).

EGG CRACKING

WITH GREAT SKILL and speed, ten-year-old Isaac cracked an egg, pulled the shell apart, and dumped the contents into a mixing bowl using only one hand. His friend Haley exclaimed, "Why did you crack the egg that way?"

My son, Isaac, replied bluntly, "Because that's how you crack an egg."

I had to smile. He had watched me. That's how I do it.

When my daughter, Cassie, was a little girl, she was helping my mom clean. She swept the dirt into a pile and laid the dustpan next to it. With her foot, she lifted the handle and held the dustpan at an angle while she swept the dirt into it. My mom was amused, knowing where Cassie had learned the technique. Once again, that's how I do it.

I wonder how many things my kids do differently because

they've watched me with one arm. I don't notice. Isaac and Cassie probably don't notice. Others may notice.

It makes me wonder, too, how many things *beyond* daily tasks they do differently because they've watched me. Things that are much more important. Things of the heart. Things that I aspire to:

Like respecting other people—older people, people with skin that isn't white, people who don't speak English, people who have mental limitations, people with physical imperfections. Have my kids seen "that's how I do it?" I hope so.

Like honoring our country—appreciating past and present sacrifices, realizing our blessings, being willing to fight for freedom. Have my kids seen "that's how I do it?" I hope so.

Like loving God—knowing Him as a friend, depending on Him for little things and big things, living out His plan for life. Have my kids seen "that's how I do it?" I hope so.

Anyway, if you ever see Isaac or Cassie do something weird, just know they learned it from me.

—◈◈◈—

"Set an example for the believers in speech,
in life, in love, in faith and in purity"
(1 Timothy 4:12 NIV).

—◈◈◈—

THE JOKE'S ON YOU

MY KIDS AND I were out for a fun day of shopping at the mall in Florence, Kentucky. Isaac, twelve at the time, had bought a coat at the Gap. He was carrying the bag with string handles across his shoulders, like a backpack. Cassie, sixteen at the time, had found some pj's at JC Penney's and we were checking out.

Jeremy was running the register. We didn't know Jeremy, that's just what his nametag said. He was a friendly guy. Lots of teenage guys were friendly when Cassie was with us. Jeremy talked nonstop while scanning the tag and taking our debit card.

In the meantime, the weight of the Gap bag became uncomfortable for Isaac so he started working to get the string handles off his shoulders. Jeremy, trying to think of the next thing to say, blurted out, "Yeah, you better get that bag off your shoulder or it will cut your circulation and your arm will fall off."

My kids' heads spun around toward me. I kept looking at Jeremy. He didn't shut up. He asked Isaac, "What's your name?" When Isaac told him, Jeremy said, "They'll start calling you one-arm Isaac."

Again my kids' heads spun around toward me. They'd never seen me chew people up and spit them out, but I think they were waiting to see if it might happen. This time I glanced at them, winked, and looked back at Jeremy. We all laughed. He thought we liked his joke. He had no idea the joke was on him.

———∽∞∾———

"God has brought me laughter, and everyone
who hears about this will laugh with me"
(Genesis 21:6 NIV).

———∽∞∾———

Cassie and Isaac (I think)

HOUSE OF HORRORS

DOWNSTAIRS IN THE family room, Cassie (seventeen at the time) and her friend Devin were beginning a girls' night of chick flicks and popcorn. Upstairs in the dining room, my husband, Tim, was taking my prosthetic arm apart to replace a broken cable.

The girls decided to go upstairs to get some drinks. They bopped through the dining room to the kitchen and grabbed a couple of Mountain Dews. Tim talked to them briefly about the movie they were watching before they headed back downstairs. Fifteen minutes later, Devin said timidly, "Uh, Cassie, can I ask you something?"

"Sure, what's up?" Cassie replied, looking at her curiously.

"What is your dad doing?"

Puzzled, Cassie asked, "What do you mean?"

Devin stammered nervously, "He has … uh … an arm on the table."

Cassie giggled. "Yeah, Mom has a prosthesis arm and Dad is working on it."

Devin's mouth dropped open. "Really! I never noticed!"

Just call our house The Alexander House of Horrors. I suppose all houses have a horror or two within. Can you identify yours? Maybe it's those forgotten leftovers in the very back left corner of your refrigerator. Maybe the friendly family mouse that always manages to evade capture. Perhaps the not-so-pleasant smell in your son's room cannot be identified. Possibly, no one dares open a closet door.

These horrors are part of our scary, marvelous, comical lives. We should enjoy them to the fullest! Take a picture of the moldy leftovers and post it on Facebook. Give your mouse a name like The Green Arrow or James Bond. Offer a reward to the family member who finds the source of the smell in your son's room. But good grief, will you clean out your closet.

---⠿⠿⠿---

"Please don't squander one bit of this
marvelous life God has given us"
(2 Corinthians 6:1 MSG).

---⠿⠿⠿---

Jingling Sound

YESTERDAY I FELL *up* the steps. I have five steps from my bedroom up to the landing in front of my bathroom and three steps from that landing up to my loft office. It happened on those last three steps. The problem is, I don't walk up steps, I run. I have always done that. There's no need to waste time on steps. But yesterday morning, my Yellow Box flip-flops tripped me, and I arrived in my office on all fours.

I hit hard. I felt nauseated. I began to evaluate the damage. Right wrist and elbow hurting a bit. Neck experiencing some pain. Left knee aching and scraped through my jeans. Left prosthetic arm making a funny jingling sound. Not good.

When I fell, I had my prosthetic arm bent at the elbow, locked into a ninety-degree angle. I landed with great force on the forearm. Had I knocked a hole in it? No. Had I cracked it? No. Had I broken the forearm from the elbow? No. Would the elbow unlock and lock into positions? Uh, oh. Normally, I had ten positions from my arm fully extended to my arm fully bent. Not anymore. I had taken out the center positions.

So I get to spend my off day today at the prosthetics facility. No offense to my friends at Fourroux Prosthetics, they are the best. The way I picture it, there's a wheel with notches and teeth inside the elbow. I think one or two of the teeth are rolling around loose. Hey, I wonder if the Fourroux team can help my bruises and pain. Probably not. I don't think they deal in flesh and blood repairs.

---◦◦◦◦---

"If the Lord delights in a man's way, he makes his
steps firm; though he stumble, he will not fall,
for the Lord upholds him with his hand"
(Psalm 37:23–24 NIV).

---◦◦◦◦---

My missing tooth

Author's note: I was right. When the team disassembled my elbow, they found a knocked out tooth. I hit hard enough to shear off three-sixteenth inches of steel!

SOUTH CAROLINA SHRIMP

OUR CHURCH STAFF was attending a one-day leadership conference in Anderson, South Carolina. When we arrived at the Holiday Inn Express on the Wednesday evening before, conference volunteers Dan and Leslie were waiting. They had a spread of delicious homemade food for us in the lounge—barbecue, potato salad, coleslaw, and chocolate chip cookies. And pounds and pounds of fresh boiled shrimp from the South Carolina coast!

I evaluated the situation. I always do that, though I don't think about doing it or even realize I'm doing it. It's an automatic action, a coping skill, an adaption talent. I thought, *Buffet line ... I'll need to balance my plate on top of my prosthetic left hand while dipping the food with my right hand. Or maybe I can find a slight open spot on the counter where I can sit the edge of my plate and lean against it while dipping. Barbecue sauce ... I might be able to get the top off the bottle. If not, I'll ask one of my coworkers to help me. Unpeeled shrimp … maybe I'll skip the shrimp. No, I really want some. I'll only get three or four. Then if I can't get the first one peeled, I'll leave them on my plate.*

As I started through the line, Dan noticed I was struggling a bit with my plate. "May I help you with that?" he asked. I gratefully accepted.

Leslie spoke up. "Does everybody know how to peel shrimp? If not, I'll show you the technique."

I admitted I didn't know how; I was going to need a lesson. Six-foot-five Dan leaned down and quietly inquired, "Would you like me to peel your shrimp?"

I smiled at him and said, "That would be great."

The food was so good, especially the shrimp. I caught myself mumbling phrases after every bite like "Oh … my … gosh, this is amazing," and "This is the best shrimp I've ever eaten."

About the time my shrimp was gone, Dan made his way to my table and asked, "Would you like more shrimp?"

I blurted out, "Yes!"

He sat at the next table, peeled a dozen shrimp, and placed them in front of me. I ate all but one, which I generously gave away. (Did I actually eat fifteen shrimp?)

I learned as much from Dan on that Wednesday evening as I did from the conference on Thursday. His actions challenged me to:

» Be on the lookout for people who are struggling.

» Offer to help them; don't wait to be asked.

» Offer quietly, not to be noticed.

» Peel shrimp for people—not just four, but sixteen!

"Never walk away from someone who deserves
help; your hand is God's hand for that person"
(Proverbs 3:27 MSG).

RESTROOM ESCAPADES

PUBLIC RESTROOMS CAN be a challenge.

First, consider sink faucets. They vary greatly from restroom to restroom. One type has a cold knob on the right and a hot knob on the left. Another type has a single lever in the center. A third type has a push button on the top.

A push-button faucet, according to advertisements, "Helps save water, energy, and money." As long as you hold the button down, the water flows freely, and when you remove your hand from the button, the water stops. To wash your left hand, you hold the button down with your right hand. To wash your right hand, you hold the button down with your left hand. When you only have one hand, how does that work? I've tried to push the button and then get my hand under the water before it stops. Occasionally, a one or two second shut-off delay will allow me to get my hand slightly wet. But most of the time, the effort is futile.

Second, think about hand-drying devices. They also come in a variety of possibilities. Remember the cloth-towel roller? Sick! Paper towel options include single-fold, C-fold, multifold, and roll dispensers. Electric dryer options include push button and hands free. Now there's a turbo dry-your-hands-in-three-seconds dryer.

The hand-drying device I dread most is a paper towel dispenser that says in bold letters on the front, Pull with Both Hands. If you pull on the center of the paper towel, a little piece tears off. If you pull on the right or the left side, you end up with a small corner of the paper towel in your hand. Clearly, you have to place your right hand on the right edge of the paper towel, place your left hand on the left edge of the paper towel, and pull down with both hands simultaneously. The bold letters might as well say, Becky—Wipe Your Hand on Your Jeans to Dry.

I know it's a little strange to get excited about public restroom equipment, but motion-sensor devices make me really happy.

"Who may ascend the hill of the Lord? Who may stand in his holy place? He who has clean hands and a pure heart" (Psalm 24:3–4 NIV).

ALABAMA HEAT

THE TEMPERATURE HAD reached ninety-one degrees on that
August day in Alabama. With the dripping humidity,
the heat index was bumping one hundred six. I usually don't
go into public places with sleeves shorter than three-quarter
length, but that day I succumbed to the heat and wore a short-
sleeved T-shirt while running errands.

The first stop on my to-do list was Gloria's Good Health
to pick up vitamins. I whipped my Toyota into a parking spot
and walked quickly into the crowded store. I had only taken
about ten steps inside the door when I heard someone exclaim
loudly, "What happened?"

I looked in the direction of the woman's voice, as did
everyone else in the store. She was gawking at me. I decided
to mess with her.

"What do you mean?" I asked, tipping my head sideways and trying to appear puzzled.

"Your arm! What happened?" the woman almost yelled.

Of course, all eyes had moved from her to me at this point.

"I was born with one arm," I tried to say nicely.

She wouldn't shut up. "Well, it looks so good!" she continued, referring to my prosthesis. "Have you learned to use it?"

"Yes," I stated bluntly. I turned and walked to the vitamin shelf, still feeling the stares of the customers.

Sometimes I just want to run errands without being the center of attention.

―――∞∞∞――――

"Many gasp in alarm when they see
me, but you take me in stride"
(Psalm 71:7 MSG).

―――∞∞∞――――

The new arm I got in 2012

A SCHOLARSHIP FOR ISAAC

L AST FALL, I had two kids in college at the same time. Yikes! I spent hours searching for scholarships and helping my son, Isaac, complete the grueling application processes. There were thousands of scholarships with every requirement imaginable: a scholarship for kids who were six feet two or taller, a scholarship for kids who were four feet ten or shorter, a scholarship for kids who were left-handed, a scholarship for kids who were a twin, a scholarship for kids with the last name of *Zolp*. I checked scholarships for Pepsi, my husband's employer, but none were available for our area. I checked scholarships for ministry, my profession, but only kids going into ministry or from certain denominations could apply. I thought of every affiliation we had and looked for scholarships related to them. Then I stumbled upon one that fit Isaac perfectly.

"Isaac, we can win this one!" I exclaimed. "It's for children of parents with disabilities."

"You're not disabled, Mom," Isaac replied.

"I know, but it says parents don't have to consider themselves disabled," I explained. "This organization, Through the Looking Glass, is doing research and just wants to hear life stories. So they're giving away sixteen, one thousand dollar scholarships!"

"Okay. What do I have to do?" Isaac asked, sounding not too thrilled at the prospect of another application.

"Write an essay about how growing up with me has affected your life," I answered. I smiled goofy, and Isaac rolled his eyes.

I jumped into action and took care of the required reference, high school transcripts, and activity resume. Isaac sat down at his Mac and began to type.

Blessings

To me, having a parent with a disability has never been an issue. Growing up and seeing my mother do incredible things without an arm has always seemed to be the norm for my family and me. Seeing my mother accomplish more than everyday tasks without so much as a doubt in her mind has made me aware that a disability has as much power as one gives it.

When I was about six, my mother, being a children's minister, was teaching the children at church about disabilities. She asked the group what they thought her disability was. At the time I was in the same group as the other children and couldn't understand what she had that was considered a disability. The only thing that came to my mind was that she had some gray hairs. I raised my hand and said so. My mother laughed. I knew that my mother had only one arm, but I never considered that a disability.

As I thought when I was six I still believe today. People are only disabled if they let something like that rule their lives. Having a mother with a "disability" has shown me how to apply this to my own life. I don't judge others by what appears to be their capacity of capability. In a way, I have almost been numbed to others' disabilities, almost being unaware of them. For instance, one day a friend and I were walking through town. My friend pointed out a man running. I noticed him running too, but my thoughts went to him being crazy for running in the summer heat. My friend's thoughts, however, went to his two prosthetic running legs. I had not even noticed that. This is just one example of how growing up with my mother has affected my views on people and disabilities and their capabilities.

I also feel my mother has taught me to have joy for all that we are given in life and to cherish what we have. I can't begin to describe the unnatural peace and joy that illuminates my mother. She has really shown me that to have joy doesn't always mean everything in life is going your way. Life is always going to find a way to get you down, one way or another. Joy is that feeling that keeps you getting up when life pushes you down. Joy is being grateful for the little things in life.

Having a mother who is strong and has never given in to her disability has forever influenced me. It has taught me to look at life in a different way and from a different perspective. I have grown up knowing that I could do anything with what I have and that I should be happy with what I have been given. I shall always be thankful for the lessons that I have been blessed with by my mother.

Isaac submitted his application packet and we waited. In November, he got a nice letter from Through the Looking Glass notifying him that he was not among those selected for a scholarship. They had received seven hundred applications!

No, Isaac didn't win the scholarship. But oh, how I treasure his essay. If his mom had been a judge, he would have won first place.

"I can do all things through Christ who strengthens me"
(Philippians 4:13 NKJV).

My Next Fifty Years

Tim McGraw has a song called "My Next Thirty Years." I'm rewriting it and calling it My Next Fifty Years.

In my first fifty years, my hair turned gray in spots, and then pink. I was pregnant seven times—two kids, five miscarriages. I went from managing nursing homes to being an executive pastor. The governor of Alabama and I led a wedding together; he performed the ceremony and I sang. I was married to a twenty-one-year-old guy, a thirty-five-year-old guy, and a fifty-year-old guy—all named Tim. I lived where I could hear fireworks when the Cincinnati Reds hit a home run. I stood on the stage of the Grand Ole Opry with Garth Brooks. So who knows what might happen in my next fifty years?

Maybe I'll help start new churches around the world. Maybe I'll travel to the final fourteen states and five continents

I haven't seen. Maybe I'll run for mayor. Maybe I'll meet Tim McGraw. Maybe I'll write *One Smile, One Arm Part 2*.

I don't know for sure what will happen, but I do know that God has a wild and wonderful plan for me. And not only for me—for you too! To experience that plan, we have to listen with our heart, be open to things outside our comfort zone, be available at a moment's notice, and be adventurous enough to follow. Along the way, if limitations threaten to slow us down or challenges attempt to stop us, we must face those head-on with courage, with determination, and with a smile.

"For I know the plans I have for you," declares
the Lord, "plans to prosper you and not to harm
you, plans to give you hope and a future"
(Jeremiah 29:11 NIV).

The main characters in One Smile, One Arm
Left to right: Tim, Cassie, Isaac, Becky, Mark,
Truby, Jeff, Sophi, Hallie, Phillip, Cindy

CPSIA information can be obtained at www.ICGtesting.com
Printed in the USA
LVOW07s0304151114

413788LV00001B/38/P